"It is time for a big bike," said Mom.

2

"I like the big red bike.
It has wide tires," said Kim.

"It is a nice bike," said Mom.
"Can you ride the big bike?" said Dad.

3

4

"I can ride the big bike fine!
The wide tires are fun!" said Kim.

"Can I tie my kite on my bike?" said Kim.
"It is not safe to ride with a kite," said Dad.

5

6 "It is time for a bike hike.
We can ride for miles and miles," said Kim.

"Ride in a line," said Mom.
"It is safe if you ride on the side," said Kim.

8

"I like my big red bike," said Kim.
"I can ride it fine, and it is mine!"